John R. Sweney

Royal Fountain, No. 3

Sacred Songs and Hymns for Use in Sabbath-School or Prayer Meeting

John R. Sweney

Royal Fountain, No. 3
Sacred Songs and Hymns for Use in Sabbath-School or Prayer Meeting

ISBN/EAN: 9783337162979

Printed in Europe, USA, Canada, Australia, Japan

Cover: Foto ©Lupo / pixelio.de

More available books at **www.hansebooks.com**

THE ROYAL FOUNTAIN,

No. 3.

SACRED SONGS AND HYMNS

FOR USE IN

Sabbath-School or Prayer Meeting,

BY

JNO. R. SWENEY AND WM. J. KIRKPATRICK.

———•———

Philadelphia: JOHN J. HOOD, 1018 Arch St.

COPYRIGHT, 1882, BY JOHN J. HOOD.

THE ROYAL FOUNTAIN.

Rescued.

MARY D. JAMES.   JNO. R. SWENEY.

Deep in the mire of sin My feet were sinking fast, And lowering o'er my head
Dark were the heavens above, Dark was the world below, No ray of light or love

Dense clouds their shadows cast; My trembling soul, o'er-whelm'd with grief, Could
To mit-i-gate my woe, Till Je-sus stooped to res-cue me, And

find no solace or re-lief, Could find no solace or re-lief.
bade my cap-tive soul be free, And bade my cap-tive soul be free.

3 Then, as an uncaged bird,
   My spirit bounded forth,—
Began to use its wings,
   And soared above the earth!
On Pisgah's summit now I rest,
In Heaven's own light supremely blest.

4 Here, on the mountain-top,
   What scenes of beauty rise!—
Bright Canaan's golden shores,
   Celestial, cloudless skies!
Enraptured with the glorious sight,
I can but *sing* for pure delight!

5 Such perfect freedom now,—
   Such light, and love, and joy!
Such fellowship divine!
   NEW SONGS my lips employ:—
How I delight his name to praise,
Who saved me by his matchless grace!

6 Now all my ransomed powers
   To God alone are given,—
A living sacrifice
   To him. On earth, in heaven,
The riches of his grace I'll sing,
To glorify my Saviour King!

Copyright, 1880, by JOHN J. HOOD.

Stand by the Blue.

W. G. T.
Wm. G. Tomer.

Soli.

1. Let those who have donned the beautiful Blue To all of their vows be faithful and true; Let's
2. Wherever we go, whatever we do, We'll keep in our mind the beautiful Blue; We'll
3. Then up and at work, keep steady in view The banner of Right, the beautiful Blue; Be

show by our lives we've all bid adieu To brandy and rum and stand by the Blue.
shun and despise in all we pursue, Both brandy and rum, and stand by the Blue.
firm in the cause, forev-er eschew Both brandy and rum, and stand by the Blue.

CHORUS.

Stand by the Blue, stand by the Blue, Stand by the Blue, by the Blue; Let's

show by our lives we've all bid adieu To brandy and rum and stand by the Blue.

Copyright, 1880, by John J. Hood.

DO RE MI FA SOL LA SI

Come to the Fountain.

Words arranged.
S. J. Robson.

1. Oh, come to the fountain when morning is breaking, And life all a-round thee is up on the wing; Oh, come, quench thy thirst up-on thy first waking At heaven's own pure, in-ex-haust-i-ble spring.
2. The Fount which above thee in freshness is gushing, Is Je-sus, the giv-er of life and of truth; While oth-ers to ru-in so mad-ly are rush-ing, Oh, give thou to him the first love of thy youth.
3. Oh, come to the fountain at noontide, while bearing The bur-den and heat of life's wear-i-some day; For Je-sus will les-sen them both by still sharing Each trouble and sorrow thou meet'st by the way.
4. Oh, come to the fountain if guilt should distress thee; 'Twas opened on pur-pose for sin-ners like thee; Here Je-sus him-self will in pi-ty address thee: "Ye poor heav-y-lad-en ones, come un-to me."

CHORUS.

Come to the fountain, the ev-er-flowing fountain, Come, for 'tis flowing still;
Come to the fountain, the ev-er-flowing fountain, Come, whoso-ev-er will.

Copyright, 1880, by John J. Hood.

DO RE MI FA SOL LA SI

STRIKE FOR GOD AND VICTORY.—Concluded.

banner; May thousands flock around it Our glorious ranks to fill.

Casting Shadows.

H. L. G.
Dr. H. L. GILMOUR.

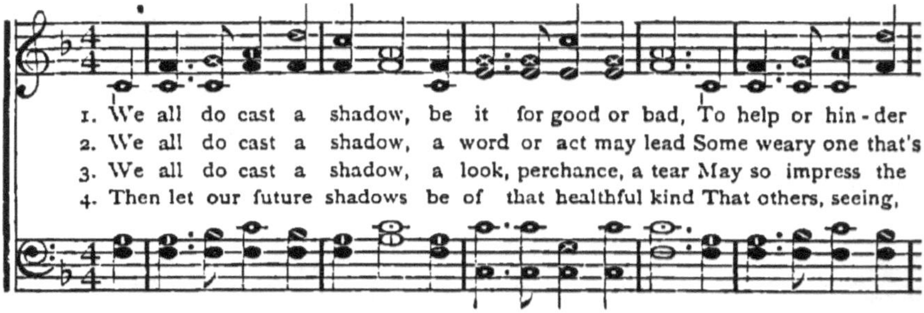

1. We all do cast a shadow, be it for good or bad, To help or hin-der
2. We all do cast a shadow, a word or act may lead Some weary one that's
3. We all do cast a shadow, a look, perchance, a tear May so impress the
4. Then let our future shadows be of that healthful kind That others, seeing,

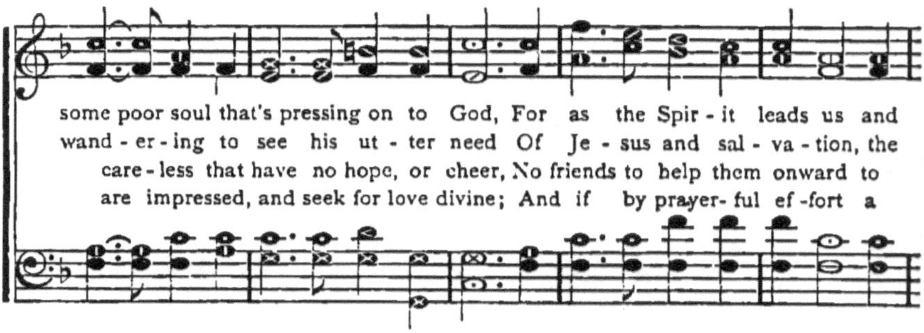

some poor soul that's pressing on to God, For as the Spir-it leads us and
wand-er-ing to see his ut-ter need Of Je-sus and sal-va-tion, the
care-less that have no hope, or cheer, No friends to help them onward to
are impressed, and seek for love divine; And if by prayer-ful ef-fort a

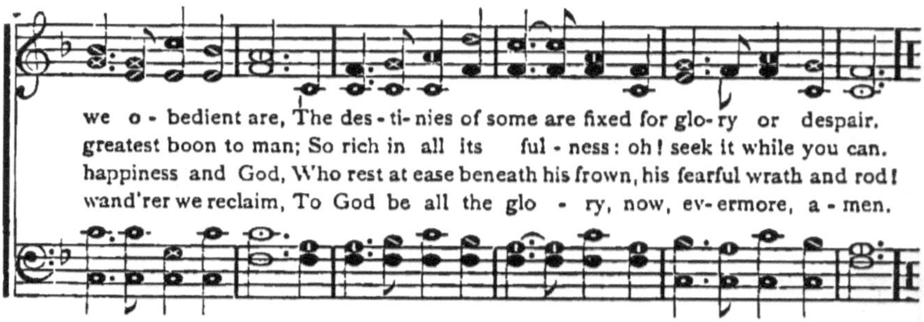

we o-bedient are, The des-ti-nies of some are fixed for glo-ry or despair.
greatest boon to man; So rich in all its ful-ness: oh! seek it while you can.
happiness and God, Who rest at ease beneath his frown, his fearful wrath and rod!
wand'rer we reclaim, To God be all the glo - ry, now, ev-ermore, a-men.

Copyright, 1880, by JOHN J. HOOD.

DO RE MI FA SOL LA SI

TOUCH NOT NOR TASTE.—Concluded.

CHORUS.

Touch not nor taste the sparkling cup, That lures to grief and pain; That woundeth like a serpent's fangs, Destroying heart and brain.

3 Go, seek them out,—poor, wand'ring sheep,
That, on the mountain cold,
Are hungry,—starving now for bread,—
Go, lead them to the fold:

There comes a cheering thought to those
Who toil in patient love,—
Each soul reclaimed shall be a star
To deck their crown above.

God is Love.

Tune, BARTIMEUS, 8, 7.

1 God is love; his mercy brightens
All the path in which we rove;
Bliss he wakes, and woe he lightens;
God is wisdom, God is love.

2 Chance and change are busy ever;
Man decays, and ages move;
But his mercy waneth never;
God is wisdom, God is love.

3 E'en the hour that darkest seemeth
Will his changeless goodness prove
From the gloom his mercy streameth;
God is wisdom, God is love.

4 He with earthly cares entwineth
Hope and comfort from above;
Every-where his glory shineth;
God is wisdom, God is love.

Copyright, 1880, by JOHN J. HOOD.

DO RE MI FA SOL LA SI

BE THOU FAITHFUL.—Concluded.

The cry is "no sur-ren-der,—Fight on and nev-er yield;"
Fill up the ranks for Je-sus, And leave no place for fear;
"Be faith-ful, fel-low sol-diers, Ye serve the King of kings,"
'Tis sweet-er than the an-gels'-song Up-on the gold-en shore.

CHORUS.

Be faith-ful, O be faith-ful, Soon ends the bat-tle strife;
O be thou faith-ful un-to death, And win a crown of life.

Key Ab. **TAKE ME AS I AM.** Tune in THE GARNER, p. 60.

1 Just as I am, without one plea,
But that thy blood was shed for me,
And that thou bidst me come to thee,
O Lamb of God, I come!

Chorus.—Take me as I am,
Take me as I am;
Oh, bring thy free salvation nigh,
And take me as I am.

2 Just as I am, and waiting not
To rid my soul of one dark blot,
To thee, whose blood can cleanse each spot,
O Lamb of God, I come!

3 Just as I am, though tossed about,
With many a conflict, many a doubt,
Fightings within, and fears without,
O Lamb of God, I come!

4 Just as I am, poor, wretched, blind,
Sight, riches healing of the mind,
Yea, all I need in thee to find,
O Lamb of God, I come!

5 Just as I am, thou wilt receive,
Wilt welcome, pardon, cleanse, relieve;
Because thy promise I believe,
O Lamb of God, I come!

Key Bb. **STAND UP FOR JESUS.** Tune, WEBB.

1 Stand up! stand up for Jesus!
Ye soldiers of the cross;
Lift high his royal banner,
It must not suffer loss;
From victory unto victory
His army he shall lead,
Till every foe is vanquished,
And Christ is Lord indeed.

2 Stand up! stand up for Jesus!
Stand in his strength alone;
The arm of flesh will fail you,—
Ye dare not trust your own;
Put on the gospel armor,
And, watching unto prayer,
Where duty calls or danger,
Be never wanting there.

3 Stand up! stand up for Jesus!
The strife will not be long;
This day the noise of battle,
The next the victor's song;
To him that overcometh
A crown of life shall be,
He with the King of Glory
Shall reign eternally.

Beautiful Hands.

Mrs. Ellen H. Gates. Jno. R. Sweney.

1. Such beau-ti-ful, beauti-ful hands, They're neith-er white nor small, And you, I know, would scarcely think That they were fair at all; I've looked on hands of form and hue A sculptor's dream might be, Yet are these a-ged, wrinkled hands Most beau-ti-ful to me.

2. Such beau-ti-ful, beauti-ful hands; Tho' her heart was weary and sad These patient hands kept toiling on That the children might be glad; I of-ten weep, as looking back To childhood's distant day, And think how these hands rested not When mine were at their play.

3 Such beautiful, beautiful hands,
  They're growing feeble now,
And tears and toil have left their mark
  On hand, and heart and brow;
Alas, alas! the nearing time,
  The sad, sad day to me,
When 'neath the daisies, out of sight
  These hands will folded be.

4 But beyond these shadowy lands,
  Where all is bright and fair,
I know full well these dear old hands
  Will palms of victory bear;
Where crystal streams through endless
  Flow over golden sands, [years
And where the old grow young again,
  I'll clasp my mother's hands.

Copyright, 1880, by John J. Hood.

DO RE MI FA SOL LA SI

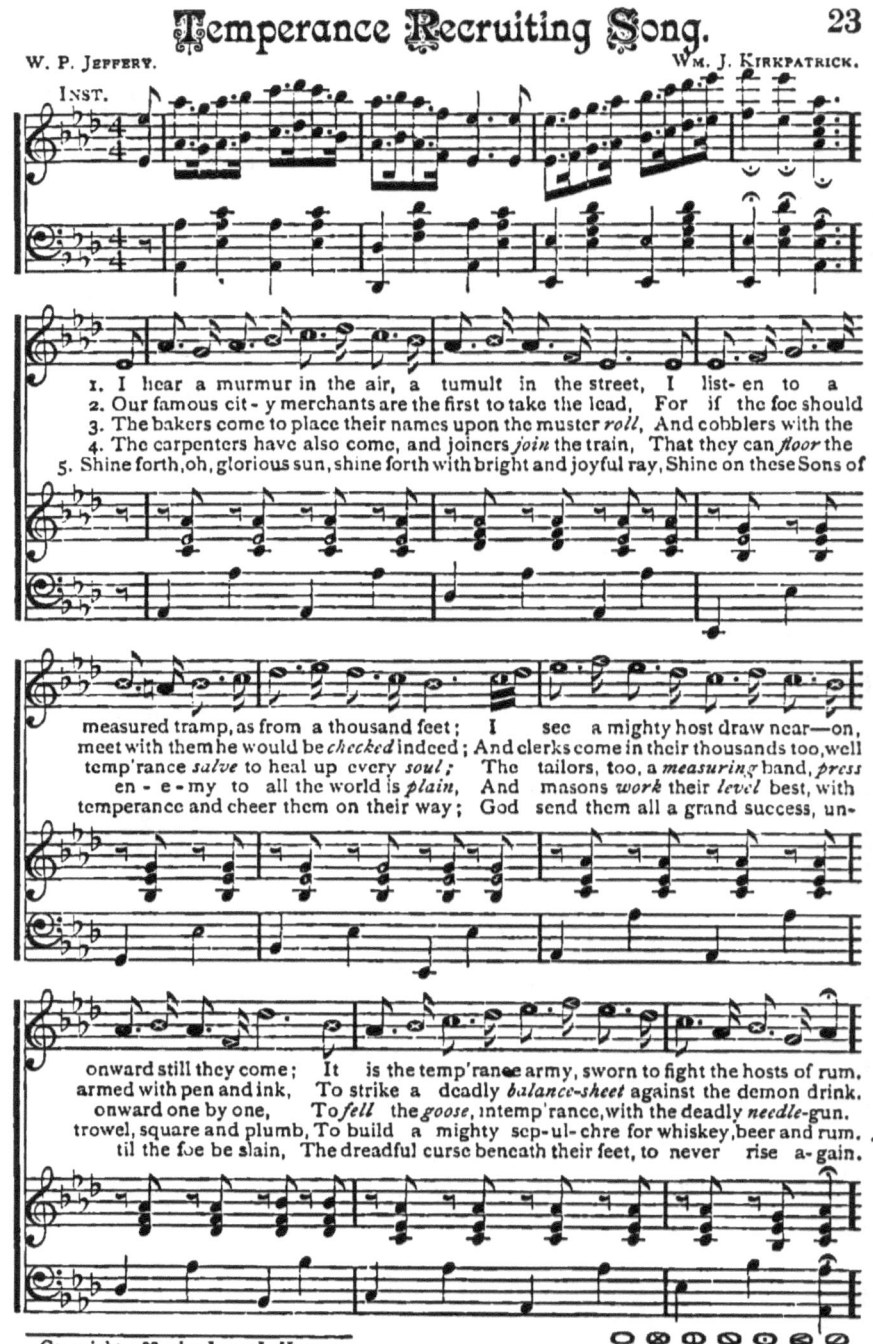

TEMPERANCE RECRUITING SONG.—Concluded.

Lift up the Latch.

Rev. E. H. Nevin, D.D.   Jno. R. Sweney.

1. 'Twas dark, and I, with inward fear, Stood like a culprit, weeping, near The
2. But in my deepest heart I knew That I had sinned, and basely too; I
3. But I would rather not comply Until my soul to mend I try; I
4. "Not now," I said, "'twill do again, When I am free from all my pain; No
5. With all my sin and guilt oppresst, With heart of stone within my breast, Dear

house in which my Saviour dwelt; Such pang my soul had never felt. A
trifled with his blood and tears, And slighted him for months and years. But
need a better heart before I could be welcome at the door: But
sighing ones are wanted there, Where songs of gladness fill the air." But
Saviour, wouldst thou honored be With guest unholy, vile, like me?" "Yes,"

Chorus.

voice addressed me from within:—"Lift up the latch, lift up the latch,
still the voice was heard within:—
said the voice that spake within,

Lift up the latch, and enter in, Lift up the latch, and enter in."

Copyright, 1879, by John J. Hood.

No Room.

Suggested by a remark made by Mr. Moody, "Supposing there was no more room in heaven."

Rev. E. H. Stokes, D. D.   Rev. J. H. Stockton.

1. It was said, and oh, I can hard-ly tell How sad-ly the news on my spir-it fell, That the heaven-ly world, all bright and fair, Was so full that no more could en-ter there, Was so full that no more could en-ter there!

2. And all through the breadth of the heaven-ly land The mansions were man-y, and great, and grand; But all were full, there was room for no more, And bolt-ed and barred was the en-trance door, And bolt-ed and barred was the en-trance door.

3 O my soul went down in deep despair,
As I said, no room—no room for me there;
No room for me there, no crown and no rest,
No fellowship sweet—for me—with the blest.

4 But soon as I turned to the word of God,
I found there was room in the Saviour's blood;
It was sin that had brought my soul in gloom,
It was sin that had said, no room, no room!

5 I found there was room since the Saviour died;
There was room—still room for the purified;
To all such, at last, a crown shall be given,
For sin, sin alone, can exclude from heaven!

6 Oh, then, to my Lord this moment I'll fly;
That I may be cleansed from sin's deepest dye,
So that when I arise from death's dark gloom,
All heaven shall cry, *there is room, still room!*

Copyright, 1880, by John J. Hood.

DO RE MI FA SOL LA SI

THE DEAD MARCH.—Concluded.

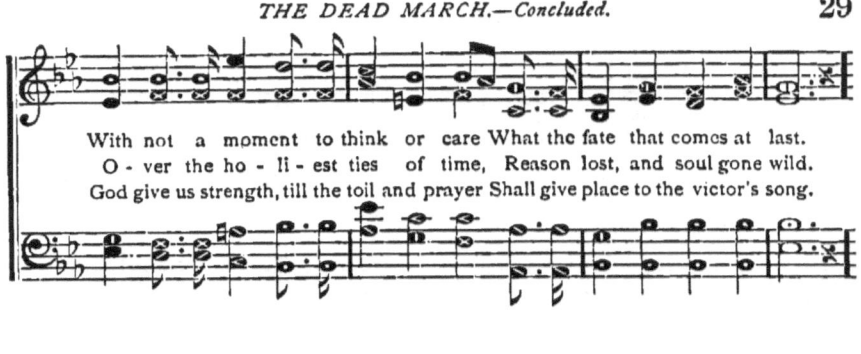

With not a moment to think or care What the fate that comes at last.
O - ver the ho - li - est ties of time, Reason lost, and soul gone wild.
God give us strength, till the toil and prayer Shall give place to the victor's song.

CHORUS.

Tramp, tramp, tramp, tramp, tramp, tramp, tramp, Tramp, tramp, tramp, tramp, What a
They are rushing mad - ly on,
tramp, tramp, tramp,

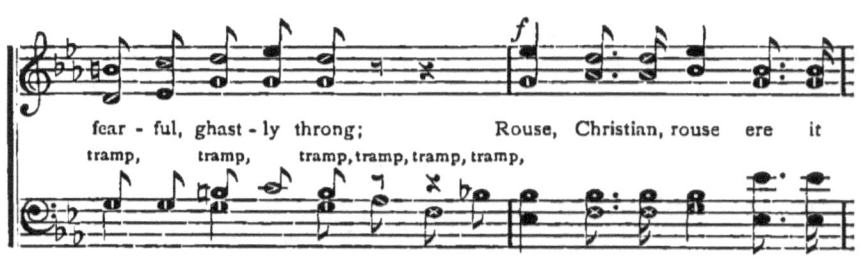

fear - ful, ghast - ly throng; Rouse, Christian, rouse ere it
tramp, tramp, tramp, tramp, tramp, tramp,

be too late, Res - cue these souls from the drunkard's fate.
tramp, tramp, tramp,

DO RE MI FA SOL LA SI

I now belong to Jesus.

"Ye are bought with a price."—1 Cor. vi. 20.

Rev. E. A. Hoffman. Wm. J. Kirkpatrick.

1. I now be-long to Je-sus! I've giv-en him my heart; No more in my af-fec-tions This world shall share a part.
2. I now be-long to Je-sus! I've giv-en him my soul; He gives me grace and cleans-ing, His blood hath made me whole.
3. I now be-long to Je-sus! I've giv-en him my all, 'Tis thine, O pre-cious Sav-iour, 'Tis thine, be-yond re-call.

D. C. I now be-long to Je-sus! I've giv-en him my heart; No more in my af-fec-tions This world shall share a part.

Key of D.

Too long my life was sin-ful, My heart too long de-prav'd;
He leads me by his coun-sel, And keeps me all the day;
O, keep me now from fall-ing, Sus-tain me by thy grace,

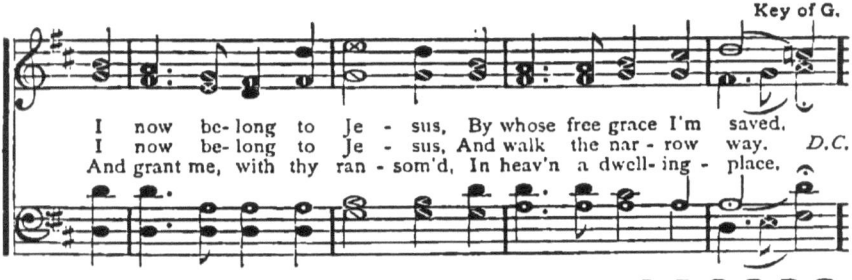

Key of G.

I now be-long to Je-sus, By whose free grace I'm saved.
I now be-long to Je-sus, And walk the nar-row way. D.C.
And grant me, with thy ran-som'd, In heav'n a dwell-ing-place.

Copyright, 1880, by John J. Hood

FAMILIAR HYMNS.

Toplady. 7s, 6 l.

1 ROCK of ages, cleft for me,
Let me hide myself in thee;
Let the water and the blood,
From thy wounded side which flowed,
Be of sin the double cure,
Save from wrath and make me pure.

2 Could my tears forever flow,
Could my zeal no languor know,
These for sin could not atone;
Thou must save, and thou alone:
In my hand no price I bring;
Simply to thy cross I cling.

3 While I draw this fleeting breath,
When my eyes shall close in death,
When I rise to worlds unknown,
And behold thee on thy throne,
Rock of ages, cleft for me,
Let me hide myself in thee.

Bethany.

1 NEARER my God, to thee!
Nearer to thee,
E'en though it be a cross
That raiseth me;
Still all my song shall be,
Nearer, my God, to thee,
Nearer to thee!

2 Though like the wanderer,
The sun gone down,
Darkness be over me,
My rest a stone,
Yet in my dreams I'd be
Nearer, my God, to thee,
Nearer to thee!

3 There let the way appear,
Steps unto heaven;
All that thou sendest me,
In mercy given;
Angels to beckon me
Nearer, my God, to thee,
Nearer to thee!

4 Then, with my waking thoughts
Bright with thy praise,
Out of my stony griefs
Bethel I'll raise;
So by my woes to be
Nearer, my God, to thee,
Nearer to thee!

Nettleton. 8s, 7s, D.

1 Come, thou Fount of every blessing,
Tune my heart to sing thy grace;
Streams of mercy, never ceasing,
Call for songs of loudest praise.
Teach me some melodious sonnet,
Sung by flaming tongues above;
Praise the mount—I'm fixed upon it—
Mount of thy redeeming love!

2 Here I'll raise mine Ebenezer;
Hither by thy help I'm come;
And I hope, by thy good pleasure,
Safely to arrive at home.
Jesus sought me when a stranger,
Wandering from the fold of God;
He, to rescue me from danger,
Interposed his precious blood.

3 O to grace how great a debtor
Daily I'm constrained to be!
Let thy goodness, like a fetter,
Bind my wandering heart to thee:
Prone to wander, Lord, I feel it,
Prone to leave the God I love;
Here's my heart, O take and seal it;
Seal it for thy courts above.

Even Me.

1 Lord I hear of showers of blesssing
Thou art scattering full and free;
Showers, the thirsty land refreshing;
Let some drops now fall on me,
Even me.

2 Pass me not, O God, my Father,
Sinful though my heart may be;
Thou mightst leave me, but the rather
Let thy mercy light on me,
Even me.

3 Pass me not, O gracious Saviour,
Let me live and cling to thee;
I am longing for thy favor;
Whilst thou'rt calling, O call me,
Even me.

4 Pass me not, O mighty Spirit,
Thou canst make the blind to see;
Witnesser of Jesus' merit,
Speak the word of power to me,
Even me.

5 Love of God, so pure and changeless,
Blood of Christ, so rich, so free,
Grace of God, so strong and boundless,
Magnify them all in me,
Even me.

Northfield. C.M.

1 O FOR a thousand tongues, to sing
   My great Redeemer's praise ;
   The glories of my God and King,
   The triumphs of his grace !

2 My gracious Master and my God,
   Assist me to proclaim,
   To spread through all the earth abroad,
   The honors of thy name.

3 Jesus ! the name that charms our fears,
   That bids our sorrows cease ;
   'Tis music in the sinner's ears,
   'Tis life, and health, and peace.

4 He breaks the power of cancelled sin,
   He sets the prisoner free ;
   His blood can make the foulest clean ;
   His blood availed for me.

Greenville. 8s, 7s, D.

1 COME, ye sinners, poor and needy,
   Weak and wounded, sick and sore :
   Jesus ready stands to save you,
   Full of pity, love and power ;
   He is able,
   He is willing : doubt no more,

2 Now, ye needy, come and welcome ;
   God's free bounty glorify ;
   True belief and true repentance,—
   Every grace that brings you nigh,—
   Without money,
   Come to Jesus Christ and buy.

3 Let not conscience make you linger ;
   Nor of fitness fondly dream ;
   All the fitness he requireth
   Is to feel your need of him !
   This he gives you—
   'Tis the Spirit's glimm'ring beam.

4 Come ye weary, heavy-laden,
   Bruised and mangled by the fall ;
   If you tarry 'till you're better,
   You will never come at all ;
   Not the righteous,—
   Sinners, Jesus came to call.

Coronation. C.M.

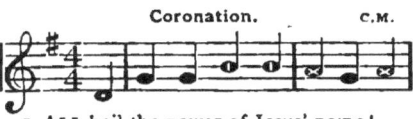

1 ALL hail the power of Jesus' name !
   Let angels prostrate fall :
   Bring forth the royal diadem,
   And crown him Lord of all.

2 Let every kindred, every tribe,
   On this terrestrial ball,
   To him all majesty ascribe,
   And crown him Lord of all.

3 O that with yonder sacred throng
   We at his feet may fall ;
   We'll join the everlasting song,
   And crown him Lord of all.

Happy Day. L.M.

1 O HAPPY day, that fixed my choice
   On thee, my Saviour and my God !
   Well may this glowing heart rejoice,
   And tell its rapture all abroad.

Cho.—Happy day, happy day,
   When Jesus washed my sins away ;
   He taught me how to watch and pray,
   And live rejoicing every day ;
   Happy day, happy day,
   When Jesus washed my sins away.

2 'Tis done, the great transaction's done—
   I am my Lord's, and he is mine ;
   He drew me, and I followed on,
   Charmed to confess the voice divine.

3 Now rest, my long divided heart :
   Fixed on this blissful centre, rest ;
   Nor ever from thy Lord depart,
   With him of every good possessed.

Martyn. 7s, D.

1 Jesus, lover of my soul,
   Let me to thy bossom fly,
   While the nearer waters roll,
   While the tempest still is high ;
   Hide me, oh, my Saviour, hide,
   Till the storm of life is past ;
   Safe into the haven guide,
   Oh, receive my soul at last.

2 Other refuge have I none,
   Hangs my helpless soul on thee :
   Leave, oh, leave me not alone,
   Still support and comfort me.
   All my trust on thee is stayed,
   All my help from thee I bring ;
   Cover my defenceless head
   With the shadow of thy wing.

3 Thou, O Christ, art all I want ;
   More than all in thee I find :
   Raise the fallen, cheer, the faint,
   Heal the sick, and lead the blind.
   Just and holy is thy name,
   I am all unrighteousness ;
   Vile, and full of sin I am,
   Thou art full of truth and grace.

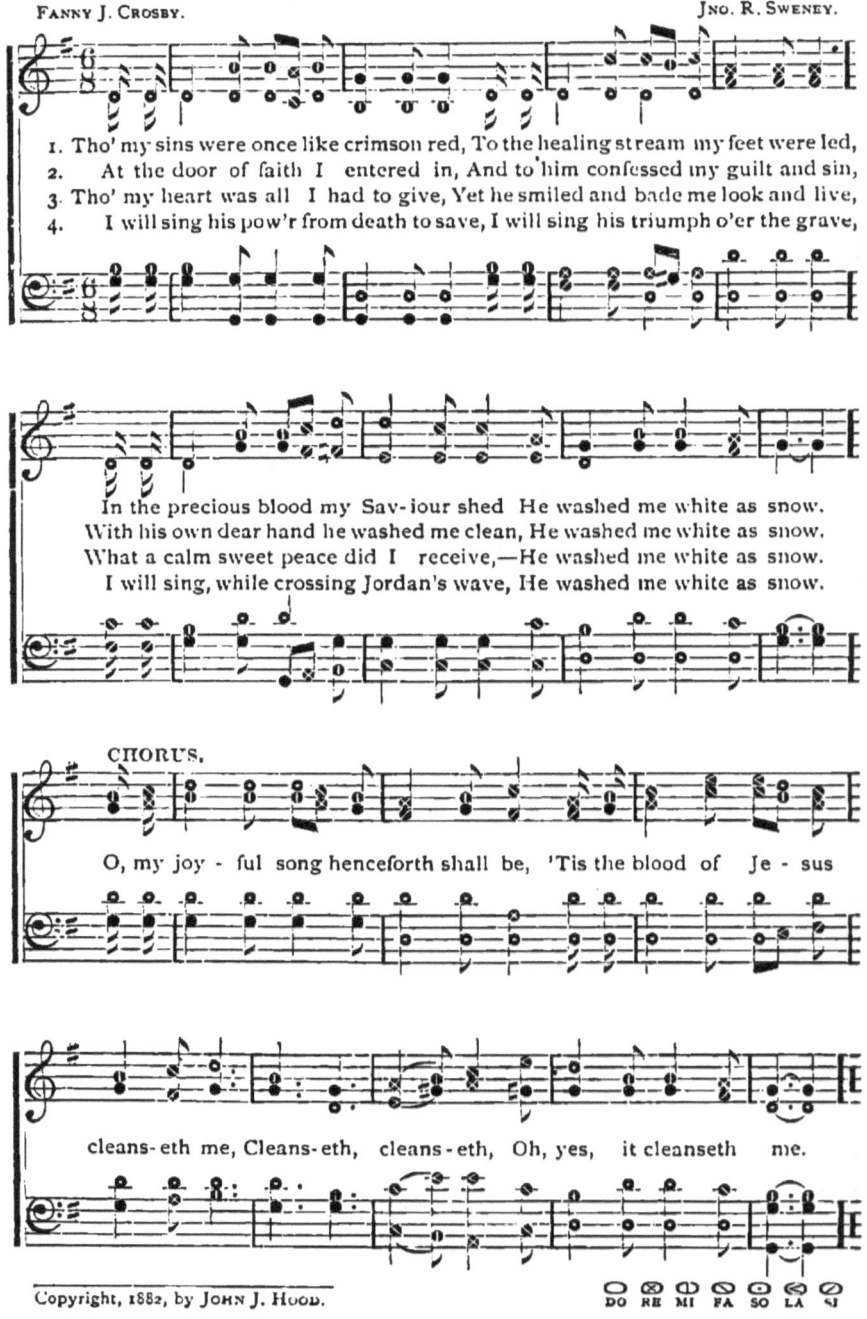

Beautiful Day.

W. J. K.
WM. J. KIRKPATRICK.

1. Beau-ti-ful day, love-ly thy light; Ho-ly each ray, ban-ishing night;
2. Beau-ti-ful day, calm was thy dawn; Joyous the lay, blessed the morn,
3. Beau-ti-ful day, perfect-ly bright; Je-sus al-way, boundless delight,
4. Beau-ti-ful day, ha-ven of rest; Ev'ry one may come and be bless'd;

Cloudless thy sky; peaceful my stay Here in the sunlight of beautiful day.
When in my heart, over my way, First shone the noontide of beautiful day.
Bliss all around, heaven by the way, Shining in fulness, oh, beautiful day.
Glory to God! naught can dismay; Christ is the light of this beautiful day.

REFRAIN.

Beau-ti-ful, beauti-ful day,   Evermore shine on my way;
Beau-ti-ful, beau-ti-ful day,   Ev-ermore shine on my way;

Saviour, I pray, keep me al-way Safe in this beauti-ful day.

beauti-ful day.

DO RE MI FA SO LA SI

By permission.

5 I know in this world I shall have tribulation;
But Jesus assures me, "in him I'll have peace;"
Then what does it matter? he is my salvation!
And sooner or later my sorrows shall cease.

6 The prospect of heaven, when life here is ended,
Gives solace in woe and a pleasure in pain;
I'll follow my Ssviour, already ascended,
And there with the ransom'd eternally reign.

Going Home Rejoicing

Fanny J. Crosby.   Jno. R. Sweney.

1. We are going home rejoicing, Where our Father's dwelling stands, We are going home rejoicing, To a house not made with hands; We are going home to Jesus, Who redeemed us with his blood, Hallelujah! hallelujah! Soon we'll cross the swelling flood.

2. We are going in a vessel That we know is firm and strong: 'Tis the good old ship of Zion That has stood the storm so long; Countless millions it has anchored, And will anchor millions more, In the port of life eternal, On the bright, celestial shore.

3. We are going home rejoicing; Praise the Lord, we're going home! Where forever and forever, With the Saviour we shall roam; Clad in robes that he has brought us,—Precious garments of his grace,—We shall see him in his glory, And behold him face to face.

CHORUS.

Soon we'll cross the swelling flood of the Jordan, And the happy, happy

Copyright, 1882, by John J. Hood.

Going Home Rejoicing.—CONCLUDED. 43

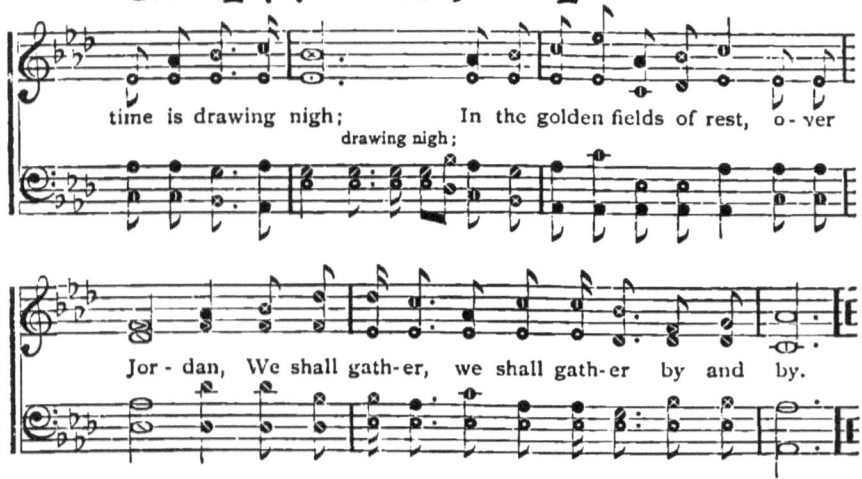

time is drawing nigh; In the golden fields of rest, o-ver
drawing nigh;
Jor-dan, We shall gath-er, we shall gath-er by and by.

Behold the Lamb of God.

FANNY J. CROSBY.   WM. CHURCH, Jr.

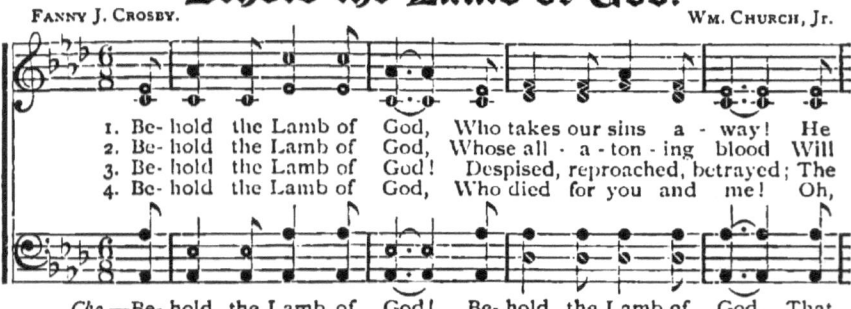

1. Be-hold the Lamb of God, Who takes our sins a-way! He
2. Be-hold the Lamb of God, Whose all-a-ton-ing blood Will
3. Be-hold the Lamb of God! Despised, reproached, betrayed; The
4. Be-hold the Lamb of God, Who died for you and me! Oh,

Cho.—Be-hold the Lamb of God! Be-hold the Lamb of God, That

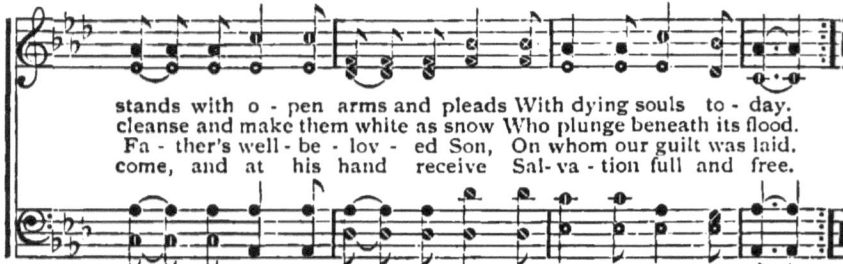

stands with o-pen arms and pleads With dying souls to-day.
cleanse and make them white as snow Who plunge beneath its flood.
Fa-ther's well-be-lov-ed Son, On whom our guilt was laid.
come, and at his hand receive Sal-va-tion full and free.

taketh a-way the sins of the world, Behold the Lamb of God.

5 Behold the Lamb of God!
   From earth's foundation slain,
That we, if faithful unto death,
   With him might live and reign.

6 Behold the Lamb of God,
   Whom now by faith we see;
Oh, tell the wonders of his grace.
   And shout redemption free.

Copyright, 1882, by JOHN J. HOOD.

DO RE MI FA SO LA SI

Dayspring.

ENGLISH.
T. C. O'KANE.

1. Come, thou "Bright and Morning Star," Light of lights, without be-ginning,
2. As the soft re-freshing dew Falls on drooping herb and flower,
3. Let thy love's pure fire de-stroy All our earth-ly taint and leaven.
4. Ah! thou dayspring from on high, Grant that at thy next ap-pearing,
5. Light us to those heavenly spheres, Sun of grace in glo-ry shrouded;

Shine up-on us from a-far, That we may be kept from sin-ning;
Let thy Spir-it shed a-new Life on ev'-ry wearied pow-er;
Kindling love and ho-ly joy With the dawning east-ern heav-en;
We who in the grave do lie May a-rise, thy summons hearing,
Lead us thro' this vale of tears To the land where days un-clouded,

Drive a-way by thy clear light Our dark night, our dark night;
Bless thy flock from thy rich store, Ev-er-more, ev-er-more;
Let us tru-ly rise ere yet Life has set, life has set;
And re-joice in our new life, Far from strife, far from strife;
Pur-est joy and per-fect peace Nev-er cease, nev-er cease;

Drive a-way by thy clear light Our dark night.
Bless thy flock from thy rich store, Ev-er-more.
Let us tru-ly rise ere yet Life has set.
And re-joice in our new life, Far from strife.
Pur-est joy and per-fect peace Nev-er cease.

Copyright, 1883, by T. C. O'KANE.

DO RE MI FA SO LA SI

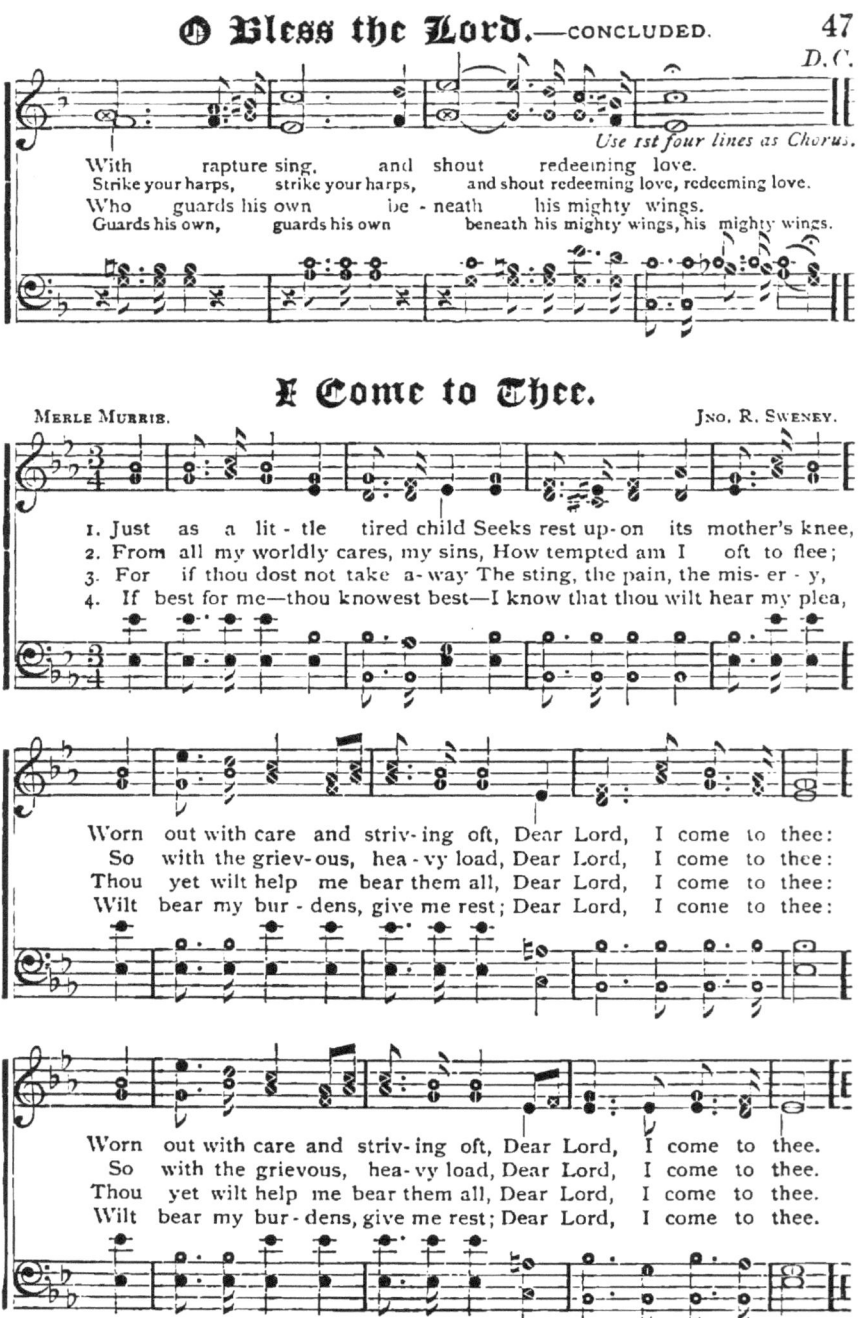

Give me Jesus.

FANNY J. CROSBY.   JNO. R. SWENEY.

1. Take the world, but give me Je - sus,—All its joys are but a name;
2. Take the world, but give me Je - sus, Sweetest com - fort of my soul;
3. Take the world, but give me Je - sus, Let me view his constant smile;
4. Take the world, but give me Je - sus; In his cross my trust shall be,

But his love a - bid - eth ev - er, Through e-ter - nal years the same.
With my Sav - iour watching o'er me I can sing, though billows roll.
Then throughout my pil- grim journey Light will cheer me all the while.
Till, with clear-er, brighter vis - ion, Face to face my Lord I see.

O the height and depth of mer - cy, O the length and breadth of love.
O the ful - ness of redemption, Pledge of end - less life a- bove.

By permission.

What of the Future?

I asked a dear one, "What of the future?" He replied, "It is all dark." —M. B. W.

Mrs. M. Bliss Wilson. Wm. G. Fischer.

1. What of the future, my broth-er,— Af-ter this world and its strife?
2. What of the future, my broth-er? Can you not see thro' the gloom
3. What of the future, my broth-er? Get thyself read-y to-night,
4. What of the future, my broth-er? Turn not a-way from the love

Is there no light for thee yon-der, Bright'ning the on-coming life?
Veil-ing the pathway be-fore you? Is it all dark in the tomb?
Fear-ing that God's Holy Spir-it, Griev-ed and sad, takes his flight.
Of the dear Saviour, who draws thee To him, and mansions a-bove.

CHORUS.

Make thyself read-y, my broth-er, Read-y to meet the dear Lord,

Knowing that soon he will call you,—Call you to meet your re-ward.

Copyright, 1883, by John J. Hood.

I shall Sleep but a Moment.

F. J. C.
Jno. R. Sweney.

1. I shall sleep but a mo-ment,—what joy will be mine When I
2. But, my Sav-iour, I ask, when on earth I must part With the
3. Thou hast nev-er desert-ed nor left me a-lone, I have
4. Shall I trem-ble to think what the strug-gle may be When the

wake in thy likeness, O Saviour divine!—When I pass from the world and its
friends I have treasured so long in my heart, That they sing me a song when my
heard its sweet mu-sic, thy life-breathing tone, When I thought the deep waters my
mandate shall come that my soul shall be free, No, I'll trust for the grace thou hast

tri-als a-way, And behold the tran-si-tion from darkness to day!
eye-lids I close, That they sing of thy love while I sink to repose.
bark would o'erwhelm, It has whispered so kind-ly, "'Tis I at the helm."
promised to give If I seek for thy hon-or and glo-ry to live.

CHORUS.

I shall sleep but a moment then wake on thy breast, A glo-ri-fied
spir-it! transport-ed and blest! And a harp, and a crown at thy

Copyright, 1882, by John J. Hood.

DO RE MI FA SO LA SI

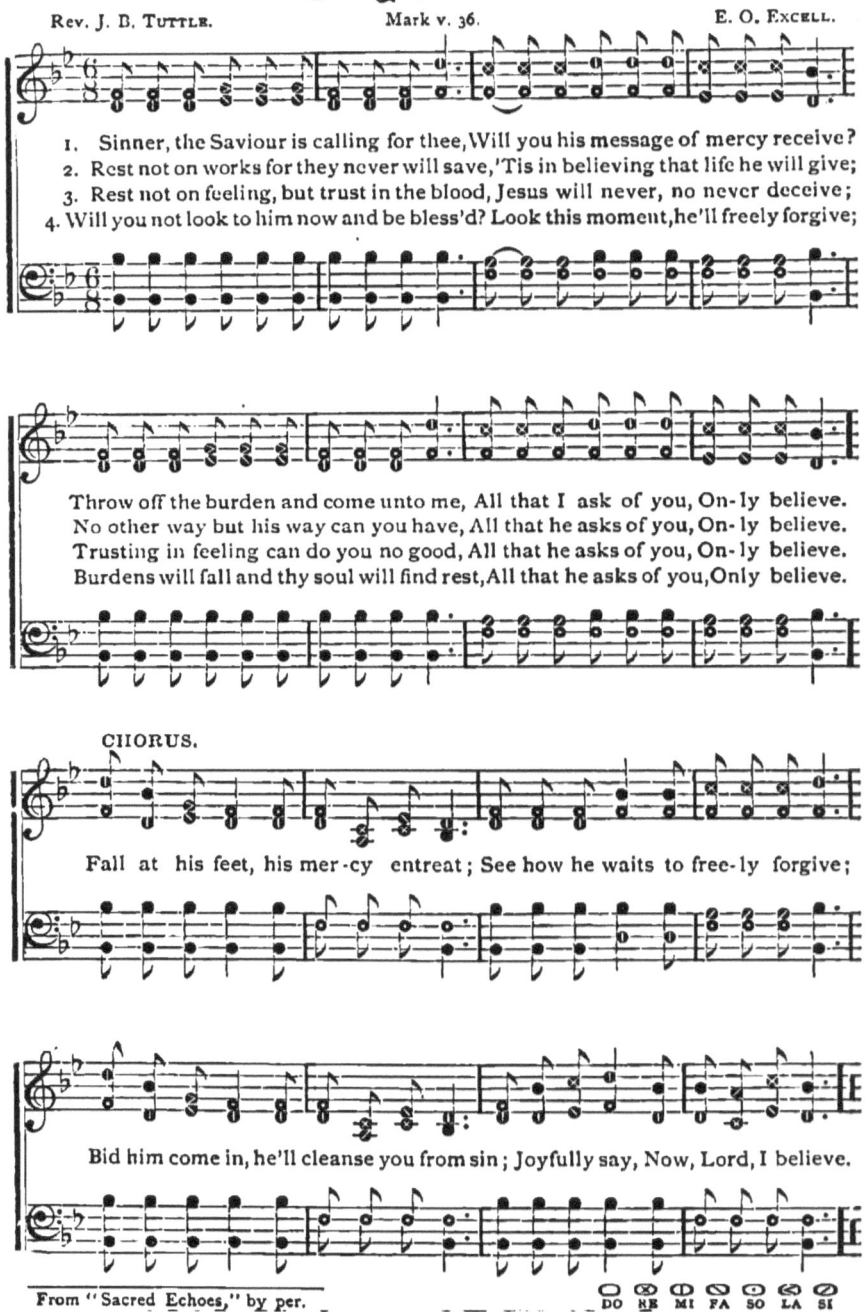

NOT FAR FROM THE KINGDOM.

Up and Away.

FRANK GOULD.   JNO. R. SWENEY.

1. Wake from thy drowsy sleep, Yonder the day, yonder the day Breaks o'er the
2. Wake from thy drowsy sleep, Time flies apace, time flies apace; Go, lest an-
3. Wake from thy drowsy sleep, List to the song, list to the song Now on the

Cho.—Wake from thy drowsy sleep, Yonder the day, yonder the day Breaks o'er the

golden fields, Up and a - way; Lose not the morning hours, Balmy and clear,
oth-er fill Thy vacant place. Speed to thy labor now, Care for thy sheaves,
summer breeze Floating a-long; Haste e'er the noon-tide beams Fall from the sky

golden fields, Up and a - way.

balm-y and clear; Toil with a cheerful heart, Reap-ing is near.
care for thy sheaves, Say, would'st thou bring thy Lord Nothing but leaves?
Fall from the sky, Work till the Mas-ter comes, Rest by and by.

Copyright, 1882, by JOHN J. HOOD.

DO   RE   MI   FA   SO   LA   SI

Land of the Blessed

Mrs. Emily Huntington Miller. T. C. O'Kane.

1. Oh! Land of the blessed, thy shadowless skies Sometimes in my dreaming I see:
   I hear the glad songs that the glorified sing Steal over eterni- ty's sea.
2. Oh! Land of the blessed, thy hills of delight Sometimes on my vision unfold;
   Thy mansions celestial, thy pal- aces bright, Thy bulwarks of jasper and gold.

Tho' dark are the shadows that gather between, I know that thy morning is fair;
Dear voices are chanting thy chorus of praise, Dear eyes in thy sunlight are fair;

I catch but a glimpse of thy glory and light, And whisper: would God I were there!
I look from my valley of shadow below, And whisper: would God I were there!

CHORUS.

Oh! Saviour, prepare . . . My spirit to share . . . For- ev- er with thee . . . those mansions fair.

3. Dear home of my Father, fair city, whose peace
   No shadow of changing can mar!
   How glad are the souls that have tasted thy joy,
   How blest thine inhabitants are!
   When weary with toiling, I think of the day—
   Who knows if its dawning be near?
   When he who hath loved me shall call me away
   From all that hath burdened me here.

By permission.

Jesus Saves.

Priscilla J. Owens. Wm. J. Kirkpatrick.

1. We have heard a joyful sound, Jesus saves, Jesus saves;
2. Waft it on the rolling tide, Jesus saves, Jesus saves,
3. Sing above the battle's strife, Jesus saves, Jesus saves;
4. Give the winds a mighty voice, Jesus saves, Jesus saves,

Spread the gladness all around, Jesus saves, Jesus saves;
Tell to sinners, far and wide, Jesus saves, Jesus saves;
By his death and endless life, Jesus saves, Jesus saves;
Let the nations now rejoice, Jesus saves, Jesus saves;

Bear the news to ev'ry land, Climb the steeps and cross the waves,
Sing, ye islands of the sea, Echo back, ye ocean caves,
Sing it softly thro' the gloom, When the heart for mercy craves,
Shout salvation full and free, Highest hills and deepest caves,

Onward, 'tis our Lord's command, Jesus saves, Jesus saves.
Earth shall keep her jubilee, Jesus saves, Jesus saves.
Sing in triumph o'er the tomb, Jesus saves, Jesus saves.
This our song of victory, Jesus saves, Jesus saves.

Copyright, 1882, by John J. Hood.

DO RE MI FA SO LA SI

86. The Rock that is Higher than I.

E. JOHNSON. WM. G FISCHER.

1. Oh, sometimes the shadows are deep, And rough seems the path to the goal,
   And sorrows, sometimes how they sweep Like tempests down over the soul.
2. Oh, sometimes how long seems the day, And sometimes how weary my feet;
   But toil-ing in life's dusty way, The Rock's blessed shadow, how sweet!
3. Oh, near to the Rock let me keep, Or blessings, or sorrows prevail;
   Or climbing the mountain-way steep, Or walking the shadow-y vale.

CHORUS.

Oh, then, to the Rock let me fly, let me fly, To the Rock that is high-er than I: is high-er than I, Oh, then, to the Rock let me fly, let me fly, To the Rock that is high-er than I.

By permission.

Come unto Me.

J. P. Mills. T. C. O'Kane.

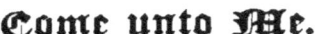

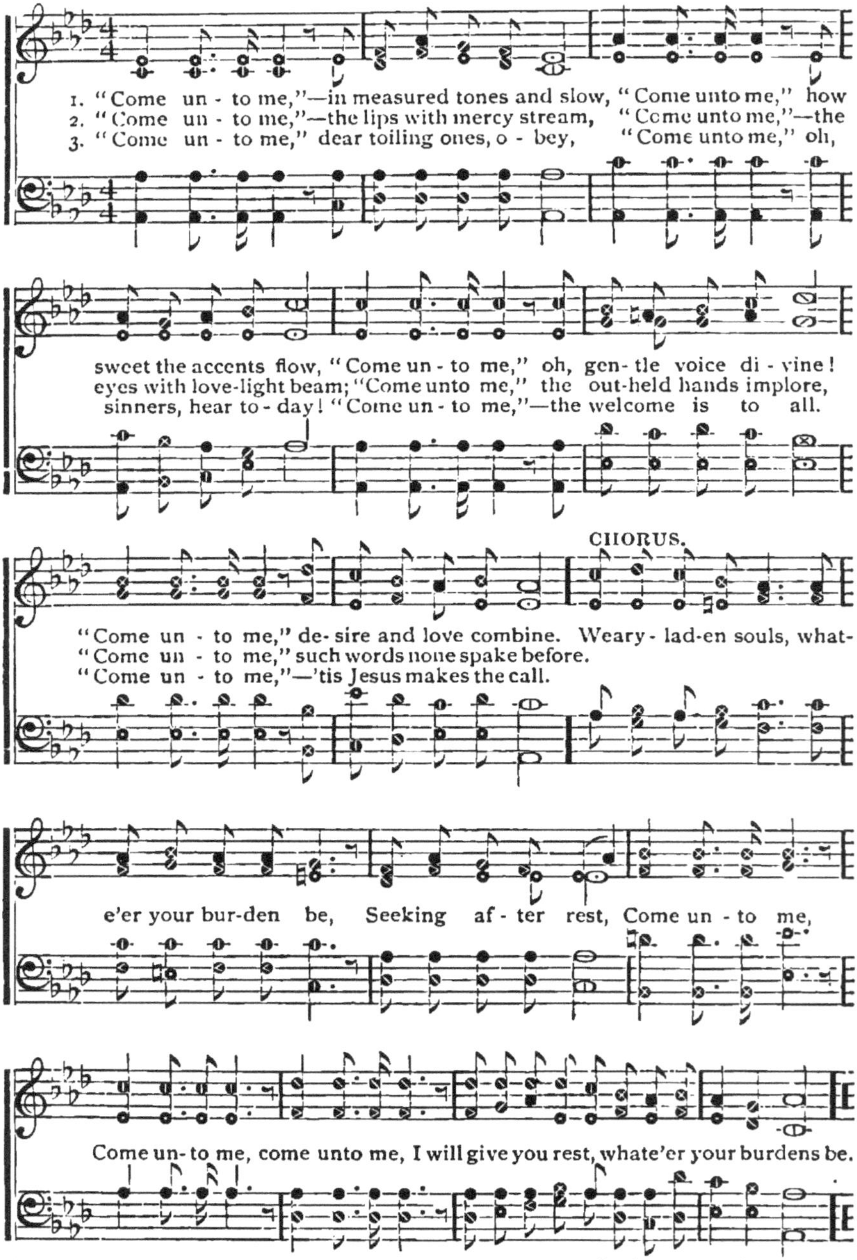

By permission.

DO RE MI FA SO LA SI

Jesus Comes.

Mrs. Phœbe Palmer. Wm. J. Kirkpatrick.

1. Watch, ye saints, with eyelids waking, Lo, the pow'rs of heav'n are shaking,
2. Lo! the promise of your Saviour, Pardoned sin and purchased favor,
3. Kingdoms at their base are crumbling, Hark, his chariot wheels are rumbling,
4. Nations wane, tho' proud and stately, Christ his kingdom hasteneth greatly,

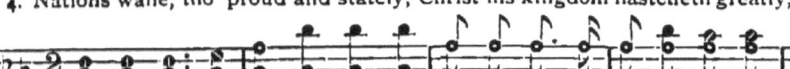

Keep your lamps all trimm'd and burning, Ready for your Lord's return-ing.
Blood-wash'd robes and crowns of glory; Haste to tell redemption's sto-ry,
Tell, O, tell of grace abound-ing, Whilst the seventh trump is sounding.
Earth her latest pangs is summing, Shout, ye saints, your Lord is coming.

REFRAIN.

Lo! he comes, lo! Jesus comes; Lo! he comes, he comes all glorious!

Je-sus comes to reign victo-rious, Lo! he comes, yes, Je-sus comes.

5 Lamb of God!—thou meek and lowly,
  Judah's Lion!—high and holy,
  Lo! thy Bride comes forth to meet thee,
  All in blood-washed robes to greet thee,

6 Sinners, come, while Christ is pleading,
  Now for you he's interceding;
  Haste, ere grace and time diminished
  Shall proclaim the mystery finished.

Copyright, 1882, by Wm. J. Kirkpatrick.

DO RE MI FA SO LA SI

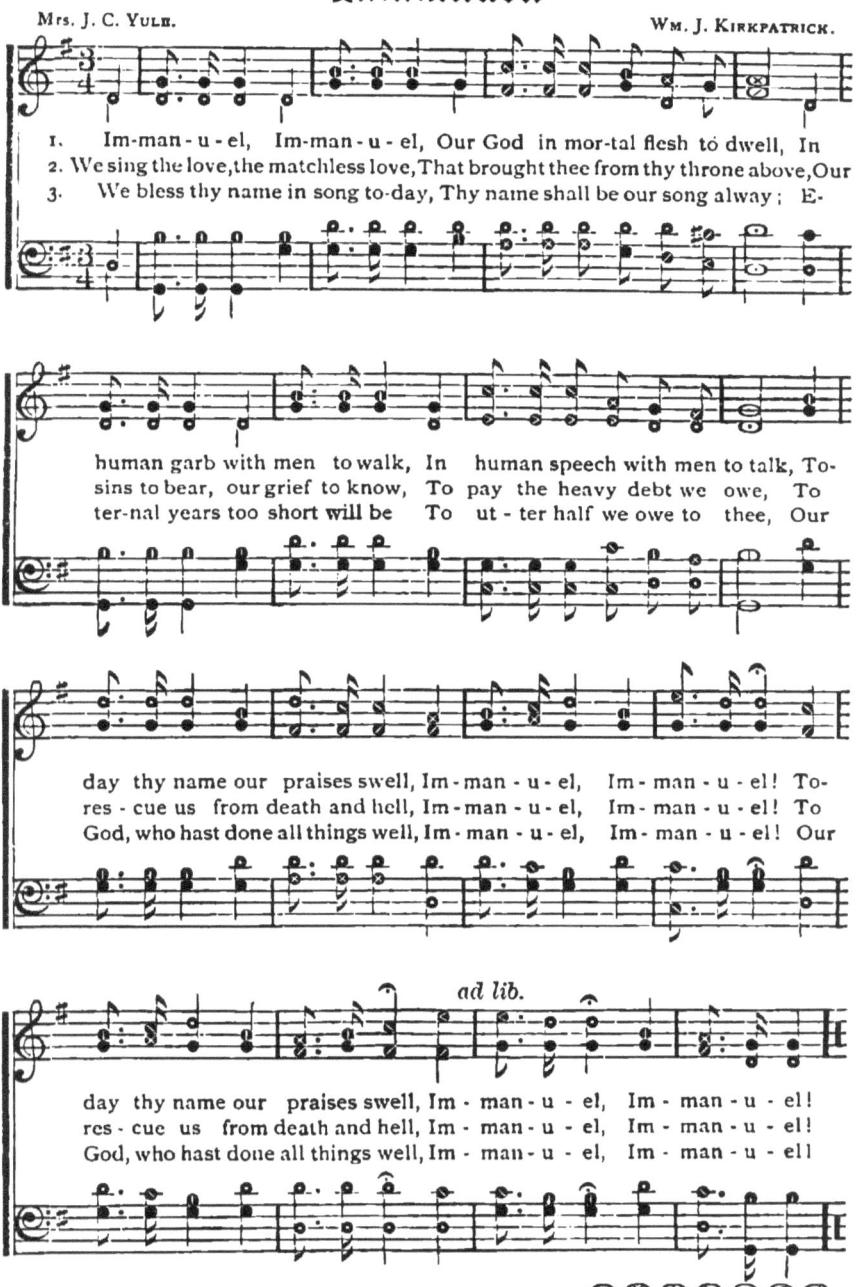

As Long as I Live.

FANNY J. CROSBY.   JNO. R. SWENEY.

1. I sing of His mer-cy, I sing of His love, Now gone to prepare me a mansion a-bove; Dear songs of my Saviour! what comfort they give! I sing and will sing them as long as I live.

2. I sing how he purchased redemption for me, How all my transgressions he bore on the tree; I sing how he whispered, thy sins I for-give, And taught me to trust him as long as I live.

3. I sing of his goodness, I sing of his pow'r, That cleanses and keeps me each day and each hour, I sing of his promise that grace he will give To shield and protect me as long as I live.

4. I sing, and with rapture my faith wings its flight To yon blissful region all love-ly and bright; Oh, there, thro' eterni-ty's a-ges that roll, I'll sing of his mer-cy, the joy of my soul.

D.S.—homeward to glo-ry I journey a-long, I'll praise my Redeem-er, I'll praise him in song.

CHORUS.

As long as I live, as long as I live, I'll praise my Redeemer, as long as I live; While homeward to glory I journey along, I'll praise my Redeemer, I'll praise him in song.

Copyright, 1882, by JOHN J. HOOD.

DO RE MI FA SO LA SI

Walking with Jesus.

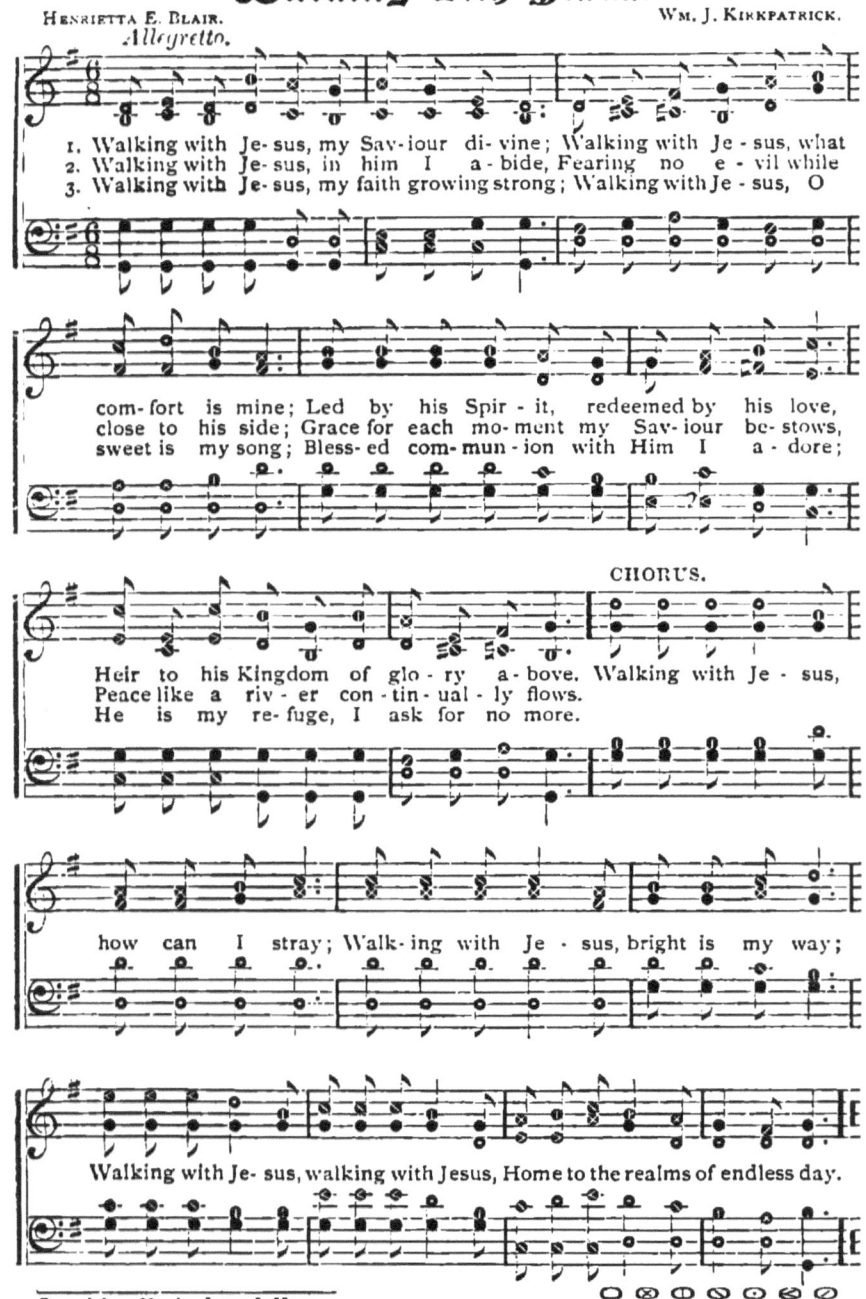

1. Walking with Jesus, my Saviour divine; Walking with Jesus, what comfort is mine; Led by his Spirit, redeemed by his love, Heir to his Kingdom of glory above.
2. Walking with Jesus, in him I abide, Fearing no evil while close to his side; Grace for each moment my Saviour bestows, Peace like a river continually flows.
3. Walking with Jesus, my faith growing strong; Walking with Jesus, O sweet is my song; Blessed communion with Him I adore, He is my refuge, I ask for no more.

CHORUS.
Walking with Jesus, how can I stray; Walking with Jesus, bright is my way; Walking with Jesus, walking with Jesus, Home to the realms of endless day.

Copyright, 1882, by JOHN J. HOOD.

Sacred Rest.

111

"For we who have believed do enter into rest."

Mrs. Mary D. James.   Heb. iv. 3.   Wm. J. Kirkpatrick.

1. How sweet the sacred rest it brings To nestle 'neath his shelt'ring wings,–The
2. 'Tis rest no angel's tongue can tell; 'Tis joy untold, unspeak-a-ble, My
3. Oh, full salvation, hallowed bliss! No creature joys compare with this Di-
4. Oh, wondrous, condescending grace! That we may bask in his bright rays, His

Lover of my soul! "A covert" from the pelting storms, "A refuge" from life's
Saviour's love to know; To see him smile, and hear him say, "I'll guide thro' all the
vine, unbroken rest:—The sacred calm the soul receives, The peace of God which
wealth of blessing prove! And lifted to the glorious height Of fellowship with

REFRAIN.

dread alarms, When raging billows roll. Oh, glo-ry be to Je-sus! How
dang'rous way Each step that thou shalt go."
Jesus gives, While leaning on his breast.
saints in light, What magnitude of love!

sweetly I am blest!—In trusting my Redeemer I am finding perfect rest.

Copyright, 1883, by John J. Hood.

DO RE MI FA SO LA SI

112 He has Come.

(Written after hearing a sermon from Chaplain McCabe, from the text, "Rejoice greatly, O daughter of Zion! Behold, thy King cometh!")

Mrs. J. H. Knowles.   Jno. R. Sweney.

1. He has come! He has come! My Redeemer has come! He has tak-en my heart as his own cho-sen home. At last I have giv-en the welcome he sought; He has come, and his coming all gladness has brought.

2. He has come! He has come! My Love and my Lord! Ev'ry thought of my be-ing is swayed by his word. He has come and he reigns in the realm of my soul, And his scep-tre is love! oh, bles-sed control!

3. He has come! He has come! O hap-pi-est heart! He has given his word that he will not depart. What trou-ble can enter; what e-vil can come To the heart where the God of all peace has his home?

4. He has come to a-bide; and ho-ly must be The place where my Lord deigns to ban-quet with me. And this is my prayer: "Lord, since thou art come, Make meet for thy presence my heart as thy home!"

CHORUS.

He has come! He has come! My Redeemer, my Redeem-er has come! His presence is heav'n, My heart is his home! My Redeemer has come!

Copyright, 1882, by John J. Hood.

Saviour, Comfort Me.

By per. Andante.   Jno. R. Sweney.

1. In the dark and cloud-y day, When earth's riches flee a-way,
And the last hope will not stay, Sav-iour, com-fort me.
2. When the se-cret i-dol's gone That my poor heart yearned upon,
Des-o-late, be-reft, a-lone, Sav-iour, com-fort me.
3. Thou who wast so sore-ly tried, In the dark-ness cru-ci-fied,
Bid me in thy love con-fide, Sav-iour, com-fort me.
4. So it shall be good for me Much af-flict-ed now to be,
If thou wilt but ten-der-ly, Sav-iour, com-fort me.

In Thy Hand.

Charlotte Elliott   T. C. O'Kane.

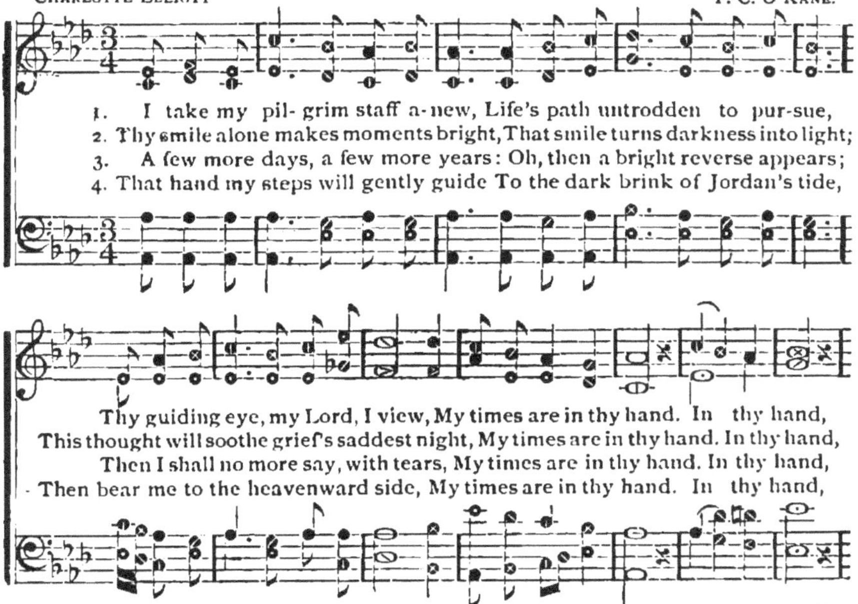

1. I take my pil-grim staff a-new, Life's path untrodden to pur-sue,
Thy guiding eye, my Lord, I view, My times are in thy hand. In thy hand,
2. Thy smile alone makes moments bright, That smile turns darkness into light;
This thought will soothe grief's saddest night, My times are in thy hand. In thy hand,
3. A few more days, a few more years: Oh, then a bright reverse appears;
Then I shall no more say, with tears, My times are in thy hand. In thy hand,
4. That hand my steps will gently guide To the dark brink of Jordan's tide,
Then bear me to the heavenward side, My times are in thy hand. In thy hand,

Copyright, 1883, by T. C. O'Kane.

DO RE MI FA SO LA SI

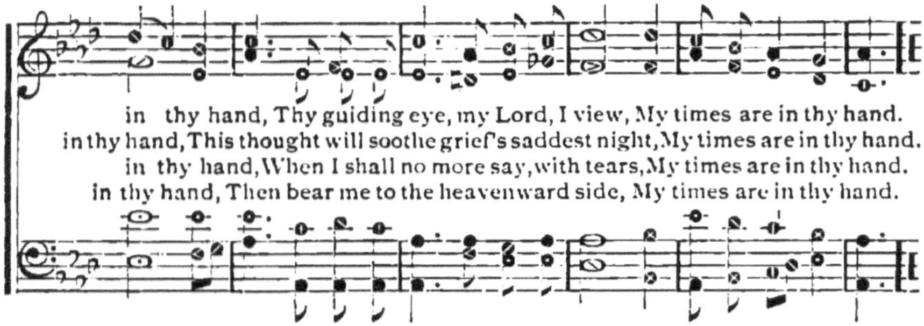

In Thy Hand.—CONCLUDED.

in thy hand, Thy guiding eye, my Lord, I view, My times are in thy hand.
in thy hand, This thought will soothe grief's saddest night, My times are in thy hand.
in thy hand, When I shall no more say, with tears, My times are in thy hand.
in thy hand, Then bear me to the heavenward side, My times are in thy hand.

Jesus Loves the Little Ones.

H. W. M.   Wm. J. Kirkpatrick.

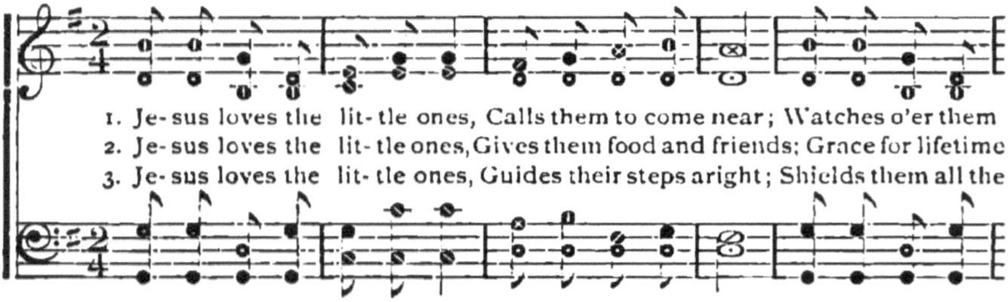

1. Je-sus loves the lit-tle ones, Calls them to come near; Watches o'er them
2. Je-sus loves the lit-tle ones, Gives them food and friends; Grace for lifetime
3. Je-sus loves the lit-tle ones, Guides their steps aright; Shields them all the

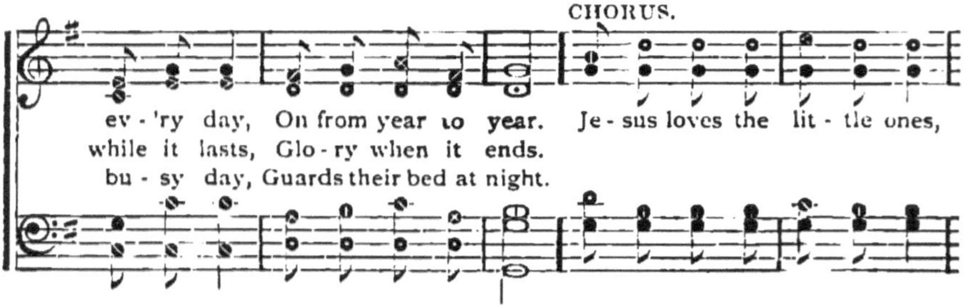

ev-'ry day, On from year to year.
while it lasts, Glo-ry when it ends.
bu-sy day, Guards their bed at night.

CHORUS.

Je-sus loves the lit-tle ones, Yes, yes, yes; All who come to him by prayer He loves to bless.

4 Jesus loves the little ones,
   Bears their sin and care;
   Loves to hear them lisp his name
   In his praise or prayer.

5 Jesus loves the little ones,
   Wheresoe'er they roam;
   Then he takes them when they die
   To his heavenly home.

Copyright, 1882, by John J. Hood.

DO RE MI FA SO LA SI

Abide with me.

Rev. H. F. Lyte.   Wm. H. Monk.

1. Abide with me! Fast falls the eventide, The darkness deepens—Lord, with me abide! When other helpers fail, and comforts flee, Help of the helpless, oh, abide with me!
2. Swift to its close ebbs out life's little day; Earth's joys grow dim, its glories pass a-way; Change and decay in all around I see; O thou who changest not a-bide with me!
3. I need thy presence ev'ry passing hour; What but thy grace can foil the tempter's pow'r? Who, like thyself, my guide and stay can be? Thro' cloud and sunshine, Lord, abide with me!
4. I fear no foe, with thee at hand to bless; Ills have no weight, and tears no bitterness; Where is death's sting? where, grave, thy victory? I triumph still, if thou abide with me!
5. Hold thou thy cross before my closing eyes; Shine through the gloom and point me to the skies; Heaven's morning breaks, and earth's vain shadows flee; In life, in death, O Lord, abide with me!

The Tranquil Hours.

Mrs. J. C. Yule.   Jno. R. Sweney.

1. The tranquil hours steal by On drowsy wings and slow, And over all the peaceful sky The stars of evening glow
2. No gath'ring clouds I see, I hear no rising blast, I fold my tired hands restfully, As though all storms were past.
3. Yet whether so or not, O Lord, thou knowest best, This night let ev'ry anxious thought And trembling fear have rest.

4. This night I will lie down
In peace beneath thine eye;
Nor heed what ills unseen may frown,
Since thou art ever nigh.

5. I will lie down to sleep,
From every terror free;
Nor wake to tremble or to weep,
Secure, O Lord, in thee!

DO RE MI FA SO LA SI

Copyright, 1882, by John J. Hood.

1882

PRICE LIST

—OF—

Church and Sabbath-School

MUSIC BOOKS,

PUBLISHED BY

JOHN J. HOOD,

1018 ARCH STREET, PHILADELPHIA.

PRICE-LIST.—MUSIC BOOKS, ETC.

	RETAIL.	PER. DOZ.
ANTHEMS & VOLUNTARIES,	$1.00	$10.00
GOODLY PEARLS, boards,	.35	3.60
THE GARNER, boards,	.35	3.60
" cloth,	.50	
" HYMN EDITION,	.12	1.20
THE QUIVER, boards,	.35	3.60
" cloth,	.50	
" HYMN EDITION,	.12	1.20
GARNER and QUIVER, Combined, bds,	.65	6.60
" " " cloth,	.75	
" " " HYMN EDITION,	.15	1.80
THE WELLS OF SALVATION, boards,	.35	3.60
MULTUM IN PARVO MUSIC LEAVES,	.40	4.20
THE ROYAL FOUNTAIN, No. 1,	.10	1.00
" " No. 2,	.10	1.00
RELIGIOUS SONGS OF THE BUELL FAMILY,	.10	1.00
SACRED ECHOES,	.10	1.00
SONGS OF MY REDEEMER,	.10	1.00
HEART SONGS,	.10	1.00
CHOIR LEAFLETS,		
No. 1. Depth of Mercy,	.10	1.00
No. 2. Come unto Me,	.10	1.00
No. 3. Praise the Lord our God,	.10	1.00
No. 4. O Lord, our Governor, etc.,	.10	1.00
No. 5. Star of the East,	.10	1.00
No. 6. Christ the Lord is risen to-day,	.10	1.00
No. 7. Daughter of Zion,	.10	1.00
No. 8. Hallelujah Chorus,	.10	1.00
FLOWER SONGS FOR DECORATION DAY,		PER 100.
No. 1. { Our Country's Loyal Brave. / Miss not a Single One,	.05	3.00
No. 2. Sweet Flowers Bring,	.05	3.00
No. 3. { They Died for Me and You, / Under the Flowers,	.05	3.00
No. 4. Come where the Pride of Columbia Rests,	.05	3.00
No. 5. { Forget not the Faithful Dead, / Peacefully Rest,	.05	3.00
SHEET MUSIC,		
A Little While to Gather Flowers,	.35	
Freedom's Flag,	.35	
Beulah Land, (Song and Chorus,)	.40	
" " (Brilliant Variations,)	.50	
One Little Empty Stocking,	.30	
SONGS OF CHEER, (Christmas Annual),	.05	4.00

TRADE DISCOUNTS: { On less than 100 books .... %
                         { On 100 books or more .... %

Announcements for 1882.

NOW READY!
THE ARK OF PRAISE,
Companion to the GARNER and the QUIVER,

By John R. Sweney and W. J. Kirkpatrick.

Price, $30.00 per 100; 35 Cts. Each

In May will be ready,

PEERLESS PRAISE:
NEW MUSIC FOR SABBATH-SCHOOLS,
WITH ELEMENTARY INSTRUCTION IN MUSIC.

By J. H. KURZENKNABE.

Price, $30.00 per 100; 35 Cents Each.

NOW READY,
THE WELLS OF SALVATION
WORDS ONLY.

Price, - $10.00 per 100.

In May will be ready,

52 HEART SONGS
Selected by C. C. McCABE,

WITH 13 POPULAR SOLOS.

Price, $18 00 per 100; 20 Cents Each.

www.ingramcontent.com/pod-product-compliance
Lightning Source LLC
Chambersburg PA
CBHW020148170426
43199CB00010B/939